MATH MATS & MORE

Hands-On Activities to Teach Early Math Skills

Preschool–Kindergarten

WRITTEN BY:
Ada Goren

EDITOR:
Jan Trautman

ARTISTS:
Theresa Lewis Goode
Sheila Krill
Kimberly Richard
Rebecca Saunders
Donna K. Teal

COVER ARTISTS:
Nick Greenwood
Kimberly Richard

www.themailbox.com

©2000 by THE EDUCATION CENTER, INC.
All rights reserved.
ISBN #1-56234-415-3

Manufactured in the United States

10 9 8 7 6 5 4 3

TABLE OF CONTENTS

ABOUT THIS BOOK

Math Mats & More is a resource book that combines the ease [of] ready-to-go reproducibles with the value of fresh, creative [tea]ching ideas. This book blends the two together to make teach-[ing] math to little ones fun and easy! In each of the 20 units in this [boo]k, you'll find

[a] reproducible math mat

[Pho]tocopy each math mat (as many times as you'd like) onto the [desi]red color of construction paper. Color the copies as desired; [the]n laminate them for durability.

[a] set of reproducible counters

[Pho]tocopy the counters onto white or colored construction paper. [Col]or them, if desired, before laminating. Cut apart the counters [bef]ore or after lamination, whichever you prefer.

[a]n idea for a center

[Mo]st of the centers in this book don't require direct supervision [onc]e you've familiarized your students with how to use them. Be [sur]e to allow students time to freely explore the mats and counters. [You]'ll be amazed at the mathematical thinking that emerges!

[a]n idea for a group activity

[The] group activities are designed for small groups of students. [The]y require some guidance from a teacher or adult helper. They [incl]ude games, songs, poems, and more.

[a] selection of math story problems

[The] math story problems are quick, easy ways to get youngsters [thin]king mathematically. Present them to small groups to assess [thei]r math skills at a glance.

[s]uggestions for alternative, three-dimensional [c]ounters to use with the mat

[So]ne are as simple as affixing theme-related mini stickers to [pen]nies. Look in your supply cabinet—you may think of other [cre]ative ideas!

Math Mats & More makes planning simple, too! Many of the [uni]ts correspond to favorite themes or holidays you already teach. [An]d if you need to reinforce a specific skill, check out the **math [skil]ls reference chart** on page 64. You'll quickly see which skills are [rein]forced by the center or group activity in each unit. And you [can] teach almost any skill at all with the math story problems [incl]uded with each mat!

[S]o make the most of your math time with *Math Mats & More*!

APPLES & BASKETS

CENTER

Apple-Pickin' Time

Harvest a crop of counting skills with this apple-picking center! In advance, prepare the mat and counters (on pages 5–6) as described on page 3. Cut out a large brown tree trunk and a green treetop. Use clear Con-Tact® paper to adhere the tree to a sheet of poster board. Then spread the apples on the treetop. (Adapt the number of apples to your students' abilities.)

To use the center, have a child pick the apples and put them in her basket. (With two or more children, have them pick the apples in turn until they are gone.) Afterward, have each child count her apples. If you have different-colored apples, encourage the children to group or graph the apples by color.

SMALL-GROUP ACTIVITY

An Apple-Pickin' Tune

Use the tree prepared in "Apple-Pickin' Time" for this musical small-group activity. To prepare, arrange a large supply of apple counters on the tree and provide one basket mat for each child. Instruct students to walk around the tree in a circle as they sing the song (right). Tell them to each pick up an apple each time they hear the word *pickin'*. Repeat the song as desired. Afterward, have each child put her apples in her basket and count them. How many apples?

I picked six apples.

MATH STORY PROBLEMS

Try these math story problems!

• "Put one apple in your basket for each person at this table." (one-to-one correspondence)

• "Put three apples in your basket. Put in two more. How many apples are in your basket?" (counting, addition)

• "Put five apples in your basket. Pretend to eat one. How many apples are left?" (counting, subtraction)

• "How many apples do you think will fit in your basket? Guess. Now fill your basket with apples. How many fit? " (estimation, counting)

(sung to the tune of "Paw Paw Patch")

Where, oh, where are all the little apples?
Where, oh, where are all the little apples?
Where, oh, where are all the little apples?
Way up high on the apple tree!

Pickin' little apples; put 'em in your basket.
Pickin' little apples; put 'em in your basket.
Pickin' little apples; put 'em in your basket.
How many apples from the apple tree?

FALLIN' FOR MORE

Autumn's bounty includes a lot more than just apples. How about these alternative counters?

• candy pumpkins
• paper or silk leaves
• small wooden apples (available at craft stores)
• apple or pumpkin mini stickers on pennies
• nuts (in the shell)

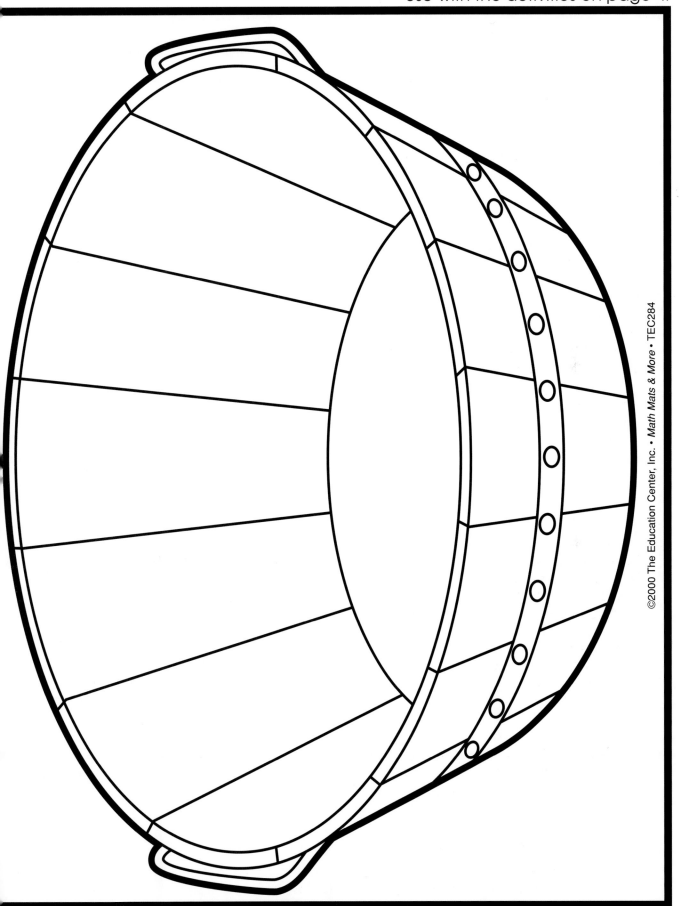

Apple Counters
Use with the activities on page 4.

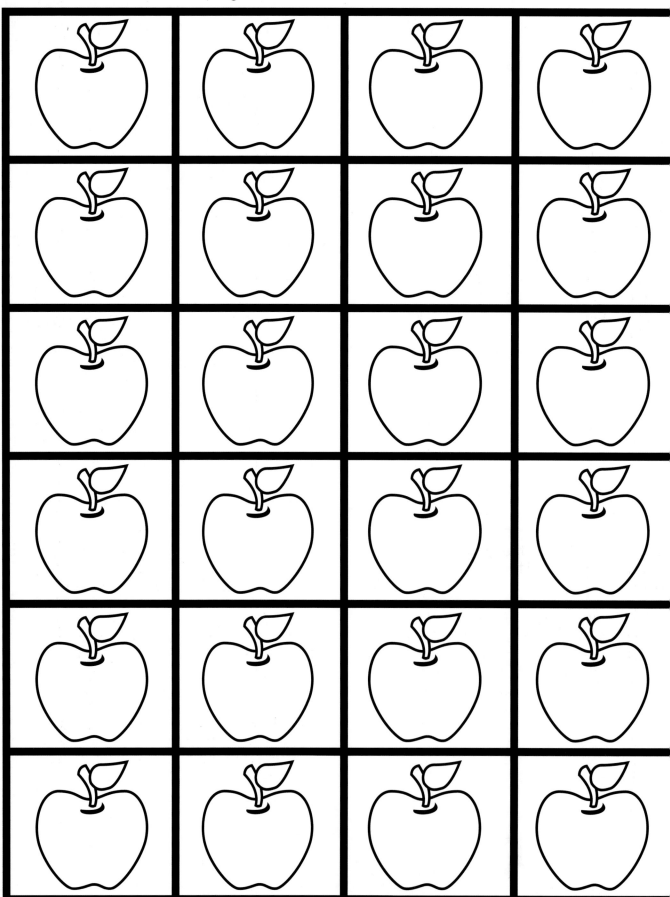

SCHOOL TOOLS

CENTER

Pack It In

Pack in those counting and matching skills with this center idea! In advance, use copies of the counters on page 9 to create several different "supply lists." (See the illustration for ideas; then adapt your lists to your students' abilities.) Also make a few copies of the backpack math mat (on page 8) and a large supply of the school tool counters (on page 9) as described on page 3. To use this center, a child chooses a supply list and a backpack. Then he counts out the number of counters indicated on his list and arranges them in his backpack. Hey—I'm ready for school!

SMALL-GROUP ACTIVITY

Ready for School!

It's a gettin'-ready race with this game of backpackin' fun! First, give each child in a small group a backpack math mat. Display one of the "supply lists" (created for "Pack It In") in the middle of the group. Stack a large supply of the school tool counters facedown near the list. Explain that the object of the game is for each child to pack his backpack to match the list and then call out "Ready for school!" To play, have each child, in turn, draw a counter from the pile. If he needs that school tool to complete his packing, he packs it in his backpack. If he doesn't need it, he mixes it in near the bottom of the pile. Keep going until someone calls out "Ready for school!" Afterward, have the remaining players sort through the pile to complete their lists, too.

MATH STORY PROBLEMS

School your little ones during small-group math times with these story problems.

- "Pack four crayons in your backpack. Now pack six pencils in your backpack. Do you have more crayons or pencils?" (counting, comparing sets)

- "Pack one crayon in your backpack. Pack one pencil. Pack one pair of scissors. Pack one ruler. How many items are in your backpack?" (counting, addition)

- "Pack eight crayons in your backpack. Take out three to share with a friend. How many are left in your backpack?" (counting, subtraction)

- "Pack three crayons in your backpack. Add two pencils and one pair of scissors. Which set has the most? Which has the fewest?" (counting, comparing sets)

MORE MATH TOOLS

You can fit a *lot* in a backpack! Try using some of these alternative counters with the backpack math mat.

- real crayons
- golf pencils
- coins (real or play)
- small sticky notes in various colors
- erasers

Backpack Math Mat
Use with the activities on page 7.

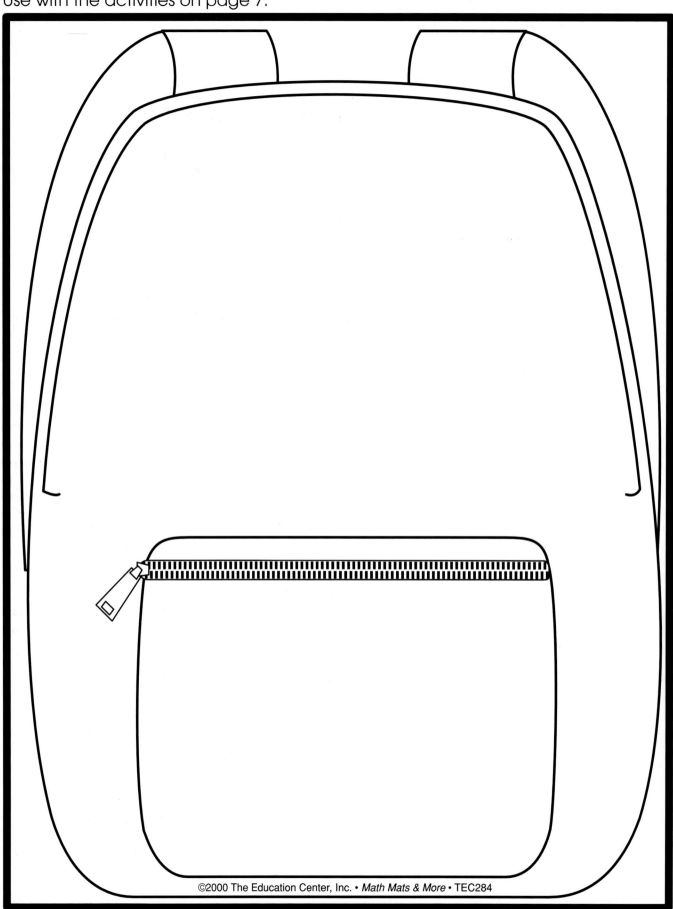

School Tool Counters

Use with the activities on page 7.

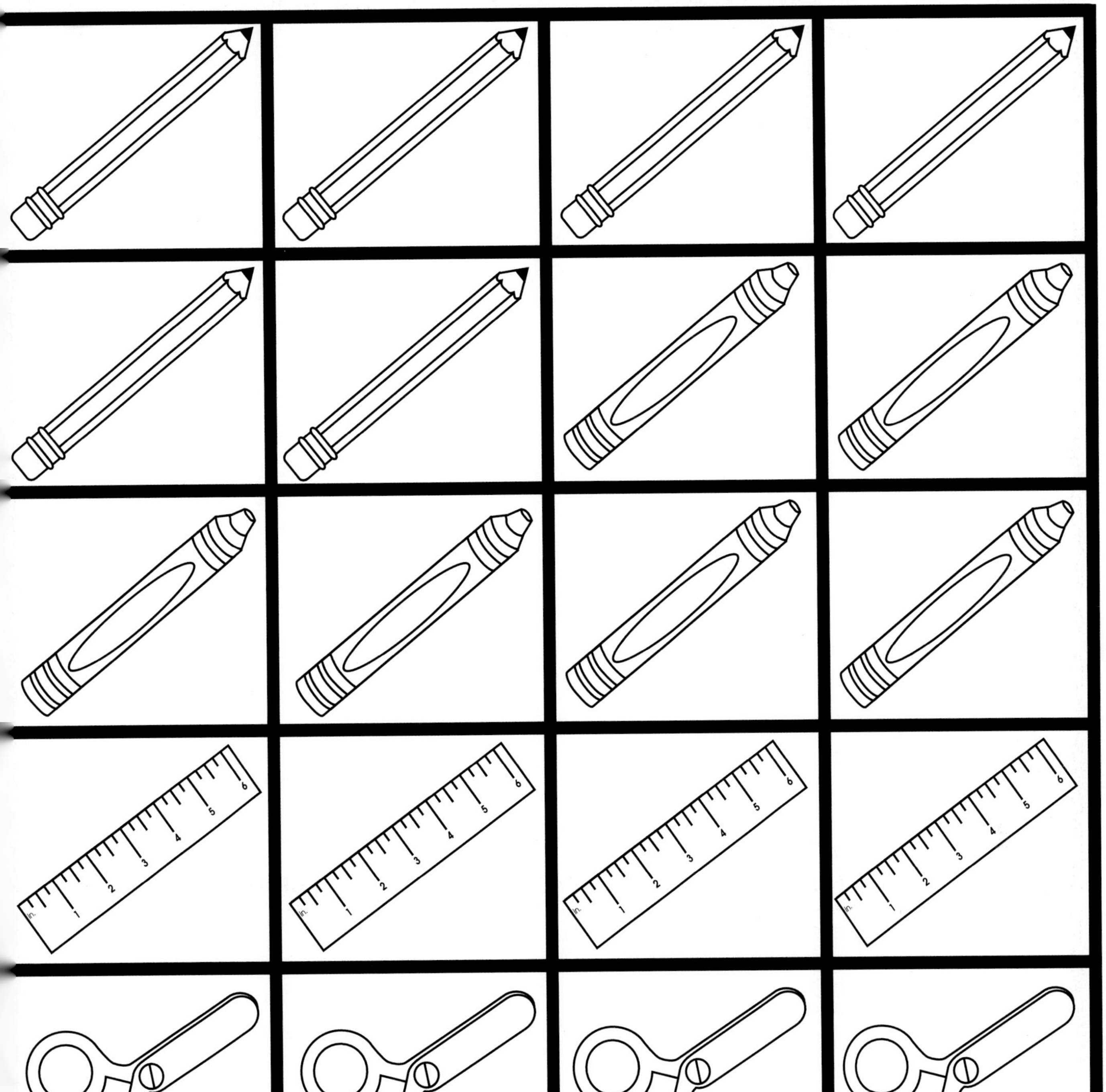

TRICK OR TREAT!

CENTER

Halloween Handfuls

Treat youngsters to this center to reinforce estimation, counting, sorting, *and* graphing skills! To prepare, make a few treat bag math mats and a large supply of candy counters (pages 11–12) as described on page 3. Store the counters in a bowl.

To use this center, have a child take a random number of treats from the bowl and place them on his mat. Ask him to estimate how many treats he has and then count to find the actual total. Encourage the child to continue his math practice by sorting his treats and arranging them to create a graph.

SMALL-GROUP ACTIVITY

Game for a Treat

Take a simulated trick-or-treat trip around the neighborhood. To prepare cut a supply of house shapes from colorful construction paper. Arrange the houses on a table along with a die. Then stack a pile of candy counters (facedown) on each house. Give each child a treat bag math mat.

To play, have each child visit each house and say "trick or treat" as she rolls the die. Have her take that many candy counters from the pile. When she has visited every house, have her sort her candy. Then how about pairing up and creating some mouthwatering patterns?

MATH STORY PROBLEMS

There's no trick to getting the most out of these math mats. Just try using them with these story problems!

- "Put four pieces of candy corn in your bag. Add six candy bars. Do you have more candy bars or candy corn?" (counting, comparing sets)

- "You go trick-or-treating. First you get three pieces of candy corn. Next, you get one piece of bubble gum. Then, you get two candy bars. How many items do you have in your treat bag?" (counting, addition)

- "How many treats will fit in your bag? Guess. Now cover your bag with treats. How many fit?" (estimation, counting)

- "Put five triangle treats in your bag. Put three rectangle treats in your bag. Do you have more triangles or rectangles?" (shapes, counting, comparing sets)

TREATS GALORE

Any of these items would make "spook-tacular" counters for use with your treat bag math mats!

- miniature candy bars
- candy pumpkins
- Halloween-themed mini erasers
- Halloween mini stickers on pennies
- candy corn
- wrapped bubble gum or sticks of gum

Candy Counters
Use with the activities on page 10.

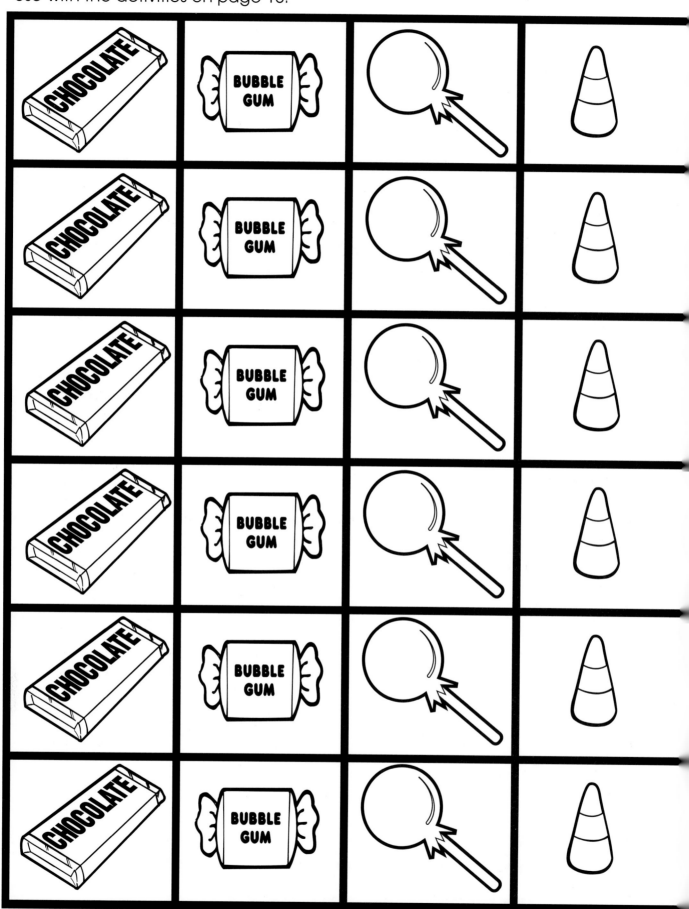

'TIS THE SEASON

CENTER

Trim the Tree

Invite students to decorate Christmas trees at this center that focuses on counting, sorting, and comparing sets. To prepare, make a few Christmas tree math mats and a large supply of colorful decoration counters (pages 14–15) as described on page 3. To use this center, have a child use the tree trimmings of her choice to decorate a Christmas tree mat. After admiring her finished creation, instruct her to sort the decorations into two piles—ornaments and candy canes. Then have her make a graph to see if she used more ornaments or more candy canes. How many of each?

MATH STORY PROBLEMS

Make your small-group math times festive with these seasonal story problems!

- "Put two red ornaments on your tree. Add one blue ornament. Now add the same number of candy canes as you have ornaments." (counting, one-to-one correspondence, addition)
- "Put a candy cane near the top of your tree. Put three red ornaments at the bottom. Put two yellow ornaments in the middle." (counting, positional words)
- "Put two green ornaments on your tree. Add four blue ornaments. How many ornaments are there on your tree?" (counting, addition)
- "Put seven candy canes on your tree. Oops! One fell off! How many are left?" (counting, subtraction)

SMALL-GROUP ACTIVITY

A Musical Match

Spread the spirit of the season as your students decorate a tree with this musical, small-group activity. To begin, give each child a tree math mat. Provide a large supply of decorations (counters) in the middle of the group. Teach youngsters the song below, naming a child in the last line. Invite that child to announce the number and type of decorations he'd like to put on his tree as he does it. Then have the other children in the group follow his directions on their own trees. Continue around the group in this manner until the trees are fully decked!

(sung to the tune of "London Bridge")

How will you trim your tree today,
Tree today, tree today?
How will you trim your tree today?
Tell us, [child's name].

I will use three blue ornaments and one candy cane!

ORNAMENT OPTIONS

Spruce up your Christmas tree math mats with some of these ideas for alternative counters.

- real mini candy canes
- wrapped peppermint discs
- small pom-poms
- large sequins
- Christmas mini stickers on pennies
- miniature wooden ornaments (available in craft stores)

Christmas Tree Math Mat

Use with the activities on page 13.

©2000 The Education Center, Inc. • *Math Mats & More* • TEC284

14

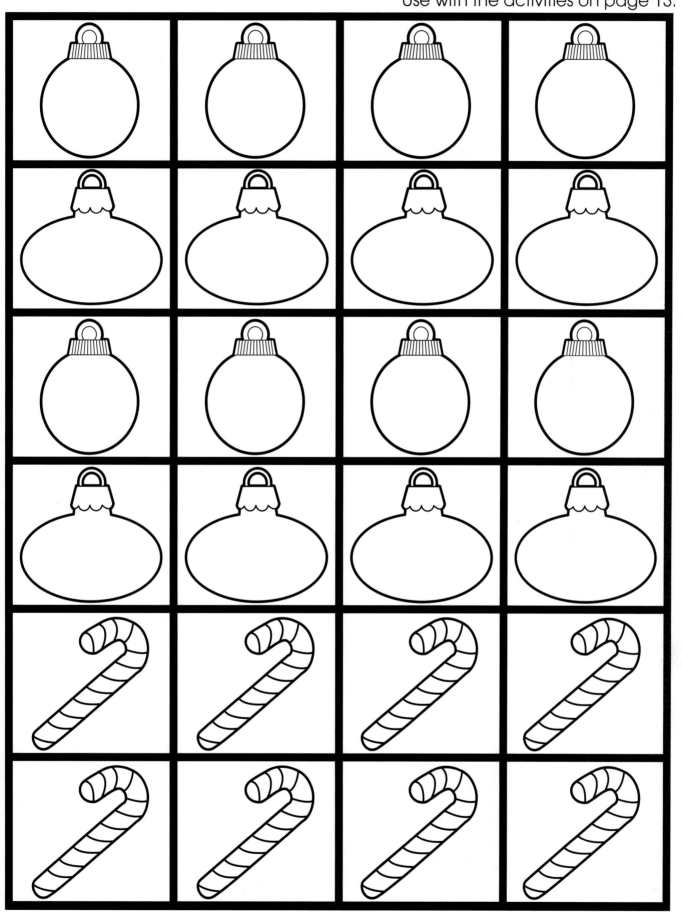

LET IT SNOW!

CENTER
Snowmen in All Sizes

Drift into lots of patterning practice with this center idea. To prepare, duplicate the snowflake and snowmen counters on page 18 to make a large supply. Use some of the copies to create patterning cards (as shown). Cut apart the remaining counters and laminate them. Also make a few copies of the snow scene math mat on page 17. Color and laminate them.

To use this center, a child chooses a patterning card. She then continues the pattern shown on the card by using the individual counters on her math mat. Also invite children to create new patterns and then copy one another's patterns.

MATH STORY PROBLEMS

Small-group math times will be a "freeze" when you use these story problems to get little ones working!

- "Put three snowmen on your mat. Point to the smallest snowman. Point to the largest snowman. Are any of your snowmen the same size?" (size identification, size comparison)

- "Put three snowflakes on your mat. Add four more. How many snowflakes are there all together?" (counting, addition)

- "Put a snowflake above the big tree. Put a snowflake beside the deer. Put a snowflake under a cloud." (positional words)

- "Seven snowflakes fell on the ground. Two melted away. How many were left?" (counting, subtraction)

SMALL-GROUP ACTIVITY
Falling Flakes

The snowflakes just keep on coming in this small-group activity! Give each child a snow scene math mat and a set of snowflake counters. Each time you repeat the chant below, insert different numbers in the first and third lines. Have youngsters use their counters to follow along. Then ask a child to count the total number of snowflakes on his mat. It's a winter wonderland!

[<u>Seven</u>] little snowflakes came out
   to play
On a cold and snowy winter's day.
Along came [<u>two</u>] more, falling free.
How many snowflakes do you see?

I see NINE snowflakes!

"SNOW" MANY COUNTERS!
Try these creative counters to make your snow scene math mats *really* cool!

- mini marshmallows
- cotton balls
- small white pom-poms
- snowflake-shaped sequins
- popped (plain) popcorn
- snowflake mini stickers on pennies

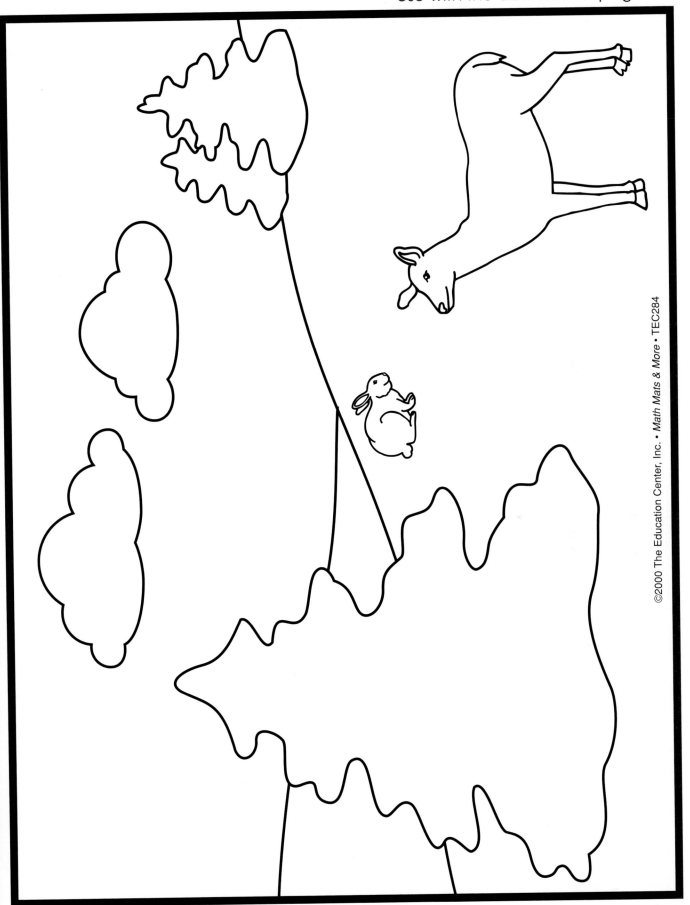

Snowflake and Snowmen Counters
Use with the activities on page 16.

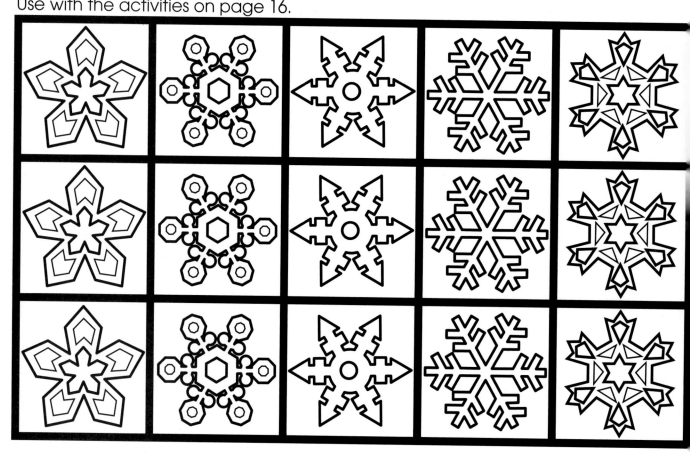

MAIL TIME

CENTER

We Deliver!

This center really delivers when it comes to numeral matching and sorting skills! To prepare, make several copies of the mailbox math mat (page 20) and a large supply of the counters (page 21) as described on page 3. Program each mailbox with a different numeral sequence to serve as an address. Program the envelopes and packages with addresses to match the ones on the mailboxes. Store all the counters in a tote bag (mailbag) at the center. To use this center, a child removes the envelopes and packages from the mailbag and delivers each piece of mail to the appropriate mailbox.

SMALL-GROUP ACTIVITY

You've Got Mail!

Little ones will be delighted to receive their own personalized mail in this small-group activity. To prepare, duplicate the mail counters on page 21 several times onto various colors of construction paper. Program each counter with a different child's name, varying the amount of mail for each child. (For younger children, glue on reduced copies of their photos.) Cut the counters apart and place them in a tote bag. During your small-group math time, ask one child to be the mail carrier. Have him take a pile of mail from the bag and deliver it to the corresponding children in the group. (He can simply set aside mail for children who are not in the group.) Then have each child count how many pieces of mail he has. Next, have all the students combine their mail and create a graph to depict letters and packages. What does the graph reveal?

MATH STORY PROBLEMS

Want to address a variety of math skills? These story problems are sure to get your stamp of approval!

- "First, you get two (red) envelopes in your mailbox. Then you get four (blue) envelopes. Do you have more (red) or more (blue) envelopes? How many more?" (counting, comparing sets)

- "You get three envelopes and two packages in the mail. How many pieces of mail do you have in all?" (counting, addition)

- "Pretend that you go on a vacation on Monday. On Monday, you get one envelope in your mailbox. On Tuesday, you get three envelopes. On Wednesday, you don't get any mail. On Thursday, you get two envelopes. On Friday, you come home and get all of your mail. How many envelopes are in your mailbox?" (counting, addition)

WHAT ELSE IS IN THE MAILBOX?
Try these alternative ideas for counters to use with your mailbox math mats.

- small valentines
- index card halves with sticker "stamps" in one corner
- envelopes from valentines with sticker "stamps" in one corner
- small wooden blocks (for packages)

Mailbox Math Mat

Use with the activities on page 19.

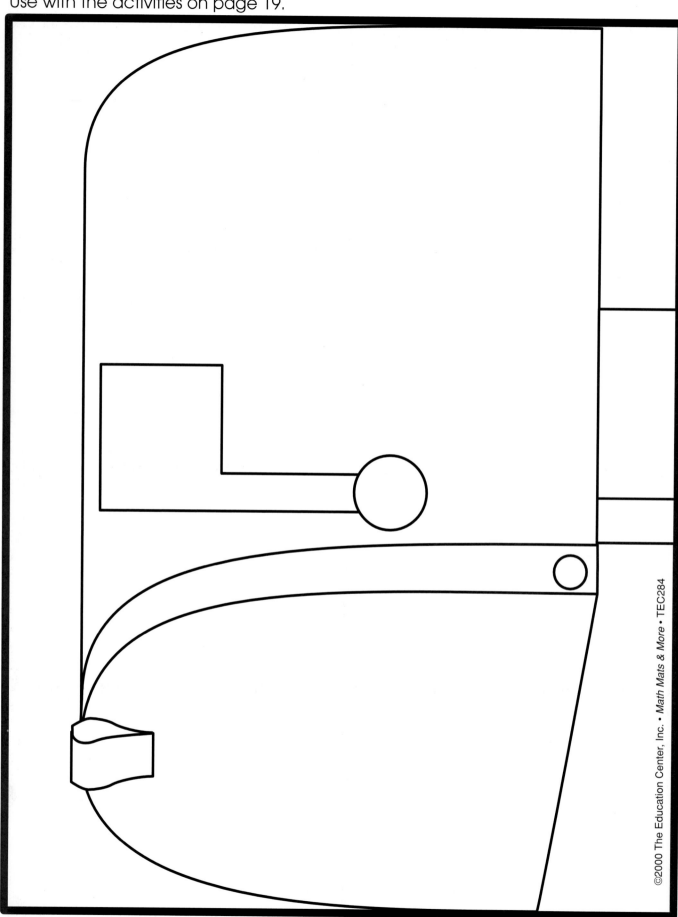

Use with the activities on page 19.

BUNNY'S BASKET

CENTER

Unscrambled Eggs

Youngsters get "egg-stra" practice with sorting skills in this center! To prepare, make three basket math mats (page 23) and a large supply of egg counters (page 24) as described on page 3. Place the mats and counters in a real Easter basket. To use this center, a child places the three math mats in front of him. He then sorts the collection of egg counters by design—dots in one basket, stripes in the second basket, and zigzags in the third.

SMALL-GROUP ACTIVITY

Bunny Delivery

Invite your little ones to hop on over for small-group math time! Give each child a basket math mat. Ask one child to be the Easter Bunny. Have her carry a real basket filled with jelly bean and egg counters as she hops around the table, counting out eight goodies for each child. Then have her take eight counters for herself and join the group. Next, recite the chant below, personalizing it for one child in the group. Have that child use her counters to determine how many goodies are left in her basket after she "nibbles" as the chant directs. Repeat the chant for each child in the group. Then really nibble on some *actual* jelly beans or chocolate eggs!

Nibble on a goodie, [child's name].
Have a little treat!
You get [three jelly beans]
To eat, eat, eat!

I have five jelly beans left!

MATH STORY PROBLEMS

Oh, goodie! Here are some story problems to make your small-group math time sweet 'n' easy!

- "Put three jelly beans in your basket. Add five more. How many jelly beans are in your basket?" (counting, addition)

- "Put eight jelly beans in your basket. Pretend to eat four. How many are left?" (counting, subtraction)

- "Put three dotted eggs in your basket. Add six striped eggs. Do you have fewer dotted eggs or fewer striped ones?" (counting, comparing sets)

- "Put five striped eggs in your basket. Make a matching set of jelly beans." (counting, matching sets)

FILL YOUR BASKET WITH MORE TREATS!

Try some of these ideas for alternative counters to use with your basket math mats.

- real jelly beans
- small foil-wrapped chocolate eggs
- malted candy eggs
- M&M's® candies in spring colors
- small fuzzy yellow chicks (available at craft stores)

Egg and Jelly Bean Counters
Use with the activities on page 22.

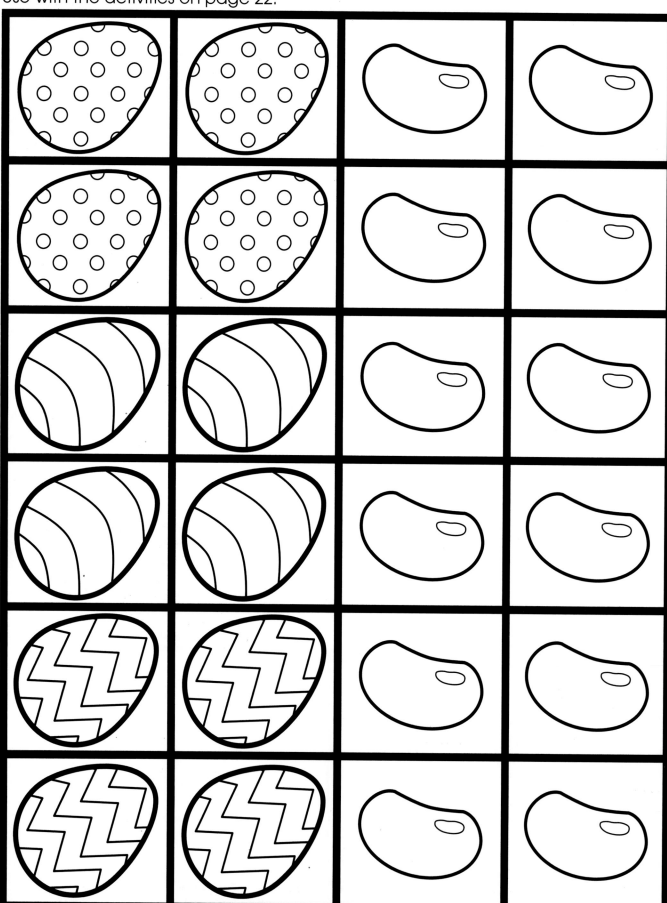

GROW, GARDEN, GROW!

CENTER

Sowing Seeds

Plant the seeds of math knowledge with this center idea. First, make several garden math mats (page 26) and a large supply of the vegetable and flower counters (page 27) as described on page 3. Next, make a supply of "seed packets." (To make a seed packet, glue a copy of a counter to an index card half. On the opposite side of the card, draw a set of seeds.) To use this center, a child chooses a mat and three seed packets. He counts the seeds on the first packet, then "plants" that many vegetables or flowers in one row of his garden. He continues planting by matching the vegetable or flower and the number of seeds shown on the remaining packets.

SMALL-GROUP ACTIVITY

Plant and Pick

Get your little gardeners counting, subtracting, and comparing sets! To prepare, make two sets of cards with the numerals 0 to 10. Separate the numeral cards into two piles—the *Plant Pile* consists of cards with numerals 6 to 10, and the *Pick Pile* has numerals 0 to 5. Give each child a garden mat and a supply of counters. In turn, each child draws a card from the Plant Pile, counts out that many vegetables or flowers, and plants them in his garden. When everyone's garden is full, each child draws a card from the Pick Pile and removes that many vegetables or flowers from his garden. When everyone has picked, have the group discuss who has the most and fewest vegetables or flowers remaining in his garden. Then play Plant and Pick again!

MATH STORY PROBLEMS

Keep small-group math times going and growing with these story problems.

- "Plant seven heads of lettuce in your garden. A hungry bunny eats two of them. How many are left?" (counting, subtraction)

- "In the top row of your garden, plant five red flowers. In the middle row, plant two blue flowers. In the bottom row, plant four yellow flowers. Which row has the most? The fewest? An equal number?" (positional words, counting, comparing sets)

- "Use two colors of flowers to make a pattern. Plant the other two rows to match." (patterning, matching)

- "Plant the following in a row: one head of lettuce, one tomato, two green beans. Which is first? Second? Third?" (ordinal numbers)

TAKE YOUR PICK!

You'll really dig these ideas for optional counters to use with your garden scene math mats!

- candy pumpkins
- large seeds (such as sunflower or pumpkin)
- large flower-shaped sequins

Garden Scene Math Mat
Use with the activities on page 25.

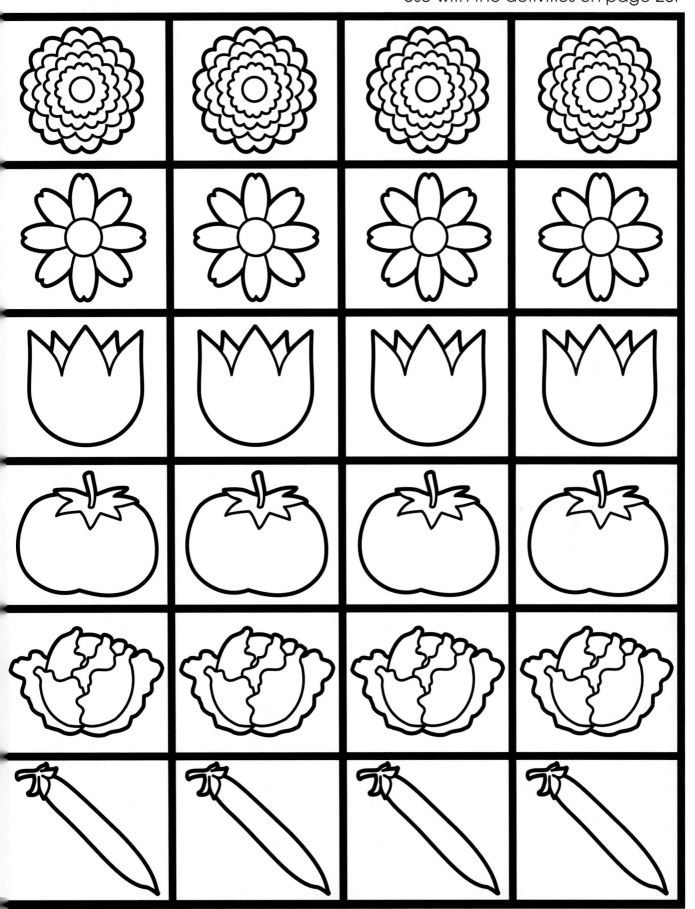

UNDER THE SEA

CENTER

See the Sea!

Invite your youngsters to visit this center to count and compare fish and shells. To prepare, make a few under-the-sea math mats (on page 29) and a large supply of the fish and shell counters (on page 30) as described on page 3. Also use one fish and one shell to make a simple recording sheet similar to the one shown. Then photocopy the recording sheet for each child. To use this center, a child places ten counters facedown on his mat. Then he turns over the counters and sorts them into two groups—fish and shells. He counts each type of counter and writes the number on the recording sheet. Then he compares the two numbers and circles the greater number. For added fun, invite youngsters to wear swim masks or goggles while they work!

SMALL-GROUP ACTIVITY

Singing Subtraction

Sing your way to subtraction practice with this small-group activity! Give each child in a group an under-the-sea math mat and a supply of fish counters. Then teach the group the song below. Each time you sing it, substitute new numbers in lines three and six. Have youngsters follow along with their fish counters; then call on a volunteer to tell you the answer.

(sung to the tune of "My Bonnie Lies Over the Ocean")

When I took a look under the ocean,
When I took a look under the sea,
I saw (seven) fish in the ocean,
Swimming by, looking at me!
Then, my oh, my oh!
(Three) swam away, swam away from me!
My oh, my oh!
How many were still there to see?

MATH STORY PROBLEMS

Dive into small-group math times with these "sea-sational" story problems!

• "Three fish were swimming in the sea. Along came six more. How many were there all together?" (counting, addition)

• "Nine fish were swimming in the sea. Four swam away. How many were left?" (counting, subtraction)

• "Put seven fish on your mat. Put six shells on your mat. Do you have more fish or more shells? How many more?" (counting, comparing sets)

• "Put a shell in the center of your mat. Put one fish above the shell. Put one fish below the shell. Put one fish to the right of the shell. Put one fish to the left of the shell." (positional words, left and right)

WHAT ELSE IS UNDERWATER?

There's lots to see under the sea! Try these ideas for alternative counters to use with your under-the-sea math mats.

- Goldfish® crackers
- small shells
- shell-shaped pasta
- Gummy fish
- small toy sea animals
- fish or shell mini stickers on pennies
- ocean-themed mini erasers

28

Fish and Shell Counters
Use with the activities on page 28.

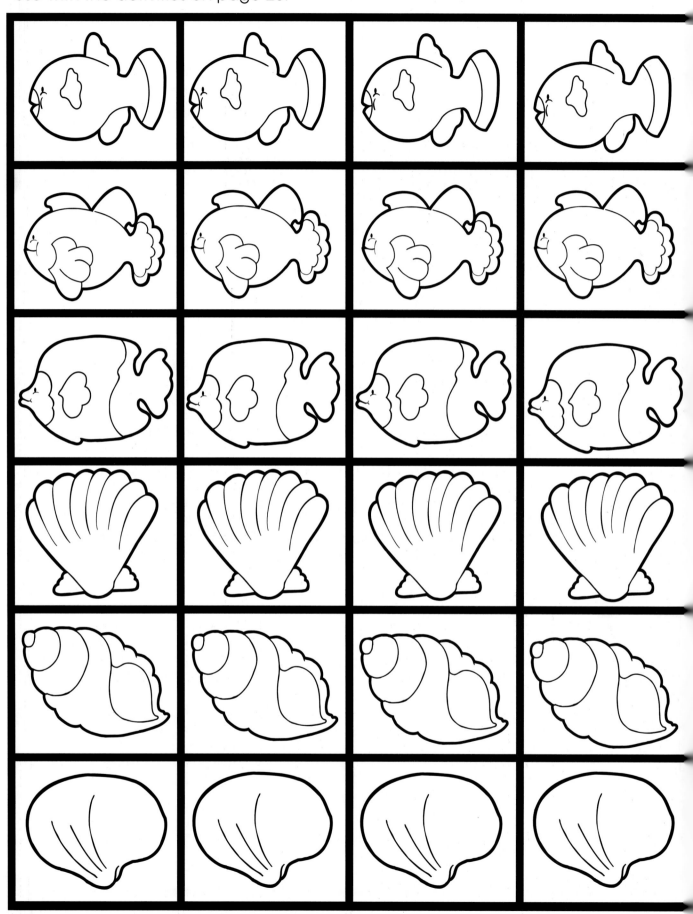

PACK A PICNIC

CENTER

Tic-Tac-Ant!

It's the red ants versus the black ants in this game that will sharpen children's reasoning skills! Prepare several copies of the picnic math mat (on page 32) as described on page 3. Also photocopy the ant counters several times to make a supply. Color half the ants red and the other half black. Then laminate the counters and cut them apart.

Have a pair of children at this center play the game in the same manner as tic-tac-toe, using the ant counters instead of Xs and Os, and the nine plates on the mat as the nine spaces on the board. Three in a row wins!

SMALL-GROUP ACTIVITY

Like Ants to a Picnic

Here's a small-group game your students will eat right up—unless the ants get to it first! To prepare, label a supply of small paper plates each with the numeral 1, 2, or 3. Stack the plates facedown like playing cards. Give each child in the group a picnic math mat and a supply of ant counters. To play, each child takes a turn flipping over a plate. She places one, two, or three ant counters (as the plate directs) on her mat, each on a different plate of food. A player is out when each plate on her mat has an ant on it. The last player to have "ant-free" food is the winner!

If desired, vary the game for older students by writing addition problems with sums of one to three on the paper plates.

MATH STORY PROBLEMS

Small-group math time will be a picnic with these story problems to get things started!

- "Put one ant on the watermelon. Put two ants on the pie. Are there more ants on the watermelon or on the pie? How many more?" (counting, comparing sets)
- "Put a matching set of ants on the chicken and on the sandwich." (counting, making and matching sets)
- "Make a parade of ants marching toward your picnic mat. Have them march one by one. Now have them march two by two, three by three, etc." (counting, making sets)
- "Ten ants came to your picnic. Three of them went to tell the rest of the colony about it. How many were left?" (counting, subtraction)

PACK THESE IN THE PICNIC BASKET, TOO!

Here are some additional ideas for counters to use with your picnic math mats.

- plastic ants or other insects
- plastic or wooden fruits and vegetables (available at craft stores)
- ant or food mini stickers on pennies
- bear counters

Picnic Math Mat

Use with the activities on page 31.

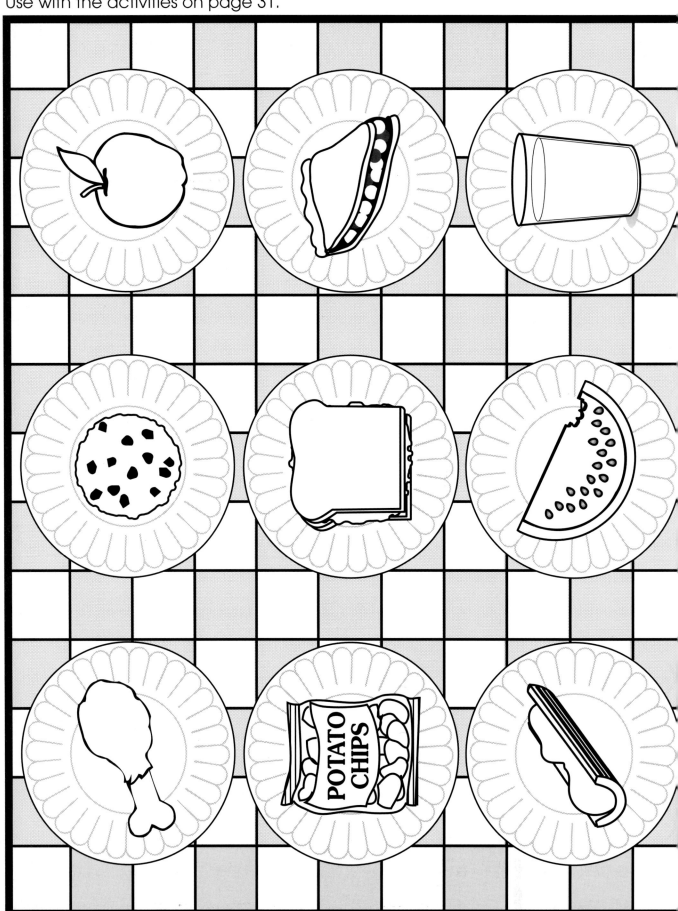

Use with the activities on page 31.

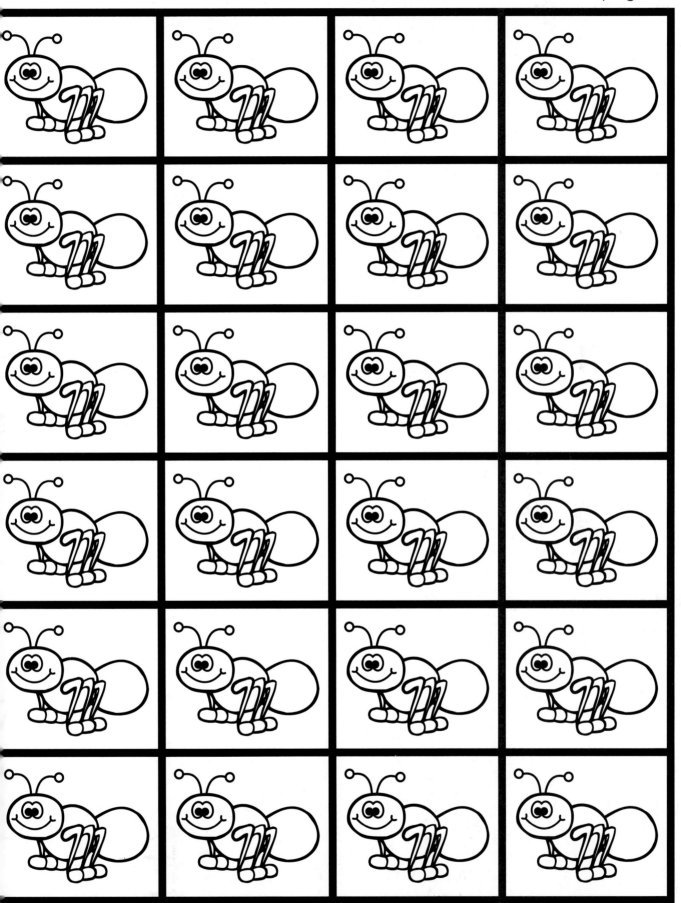

HAPPY BIRTHDAY!

CENTER

Pick a Pattern

Make patterning practice deliciously fun with this colorful center activity. In advance, prepare a few copies of the birthday cake math mat (on page 35) and a large supply of the candle and flower counters (on page 36) as described on page 3. Create a supply of patterning cards by drawing candles and flowers on unlined index cards (in colors to match the counters).

To use this center, a child chooses a mat and two patterning cards—one showing candles and one showing flowers. She uses the counters to continue the patterns on her mat—candles on top of her cake and flowers on the side. Mmm…looks good!

SMALL-GROUP ACTIVITY

Name Your Number

How old are you? Provide each child in a small group with a cake mat and a set of candle counters (including the numeral candles). Sing the song (right), filling in a different child's name each time you sing it. Invite the named child to choose a numeral candle; then have everyone in the group count that same number of candles onto his cake. Repeat the song until each child has had a turn.

Seven candles.

MATH STORY PROBLEMS

Small-group math time today? Piece o' cake! Just try these story problems to get those little minds thinking.

• "Put the number 4 candle on your cake. Put a matching number of flower decorations on the side of the cake." (identifying numerals, matching numerals and sets)

• "How many flower decorations will fit on the side of your cake? Guess. Now fill the side with flowers. How many actually fit?" (estimating, counting)

• "Your friend is four years old. Show how many candles he'll have on his cake on his *next* birthday." (reasoning, counting)

(sung to the tune of "Happy Birthday to You")

How many candles for you?
How many candles for you?
How many candles, dear [child's name]?
How many candles for you?

MORE CAKE COUNTERS

Decorate your birthday cake mats with some of these alternative counters.

• real birthday candles
• candy cake decorations
• small candles, such as M&M's® or gumdrops
• flower mini stickers on pennies
• large sequins

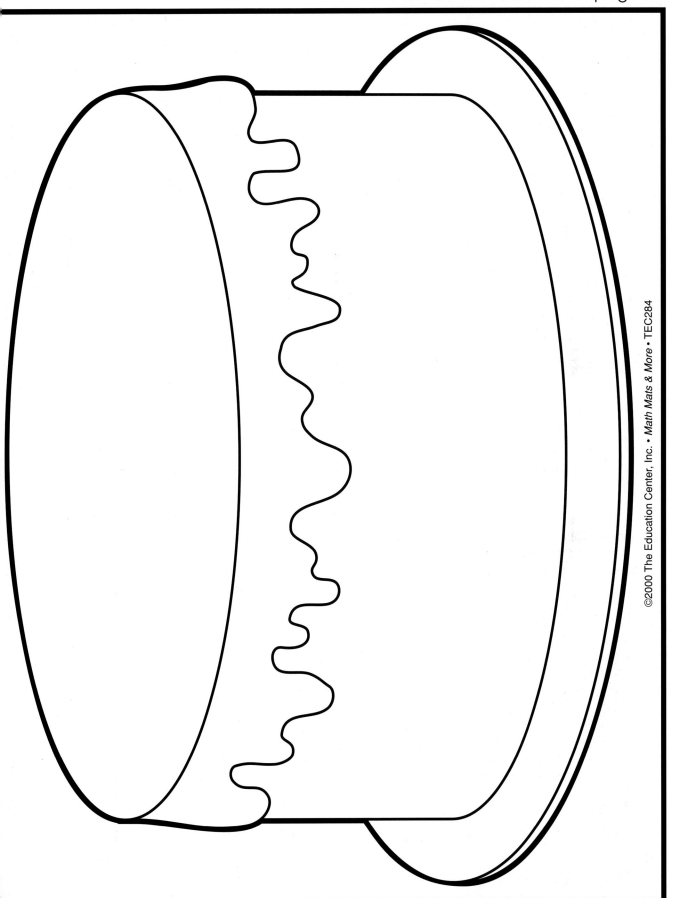

Candle and Flower Counters
Use with the activities on page 34.

FILL THE JAR

CENTER

The Candy Store

Invite little ones to this imaginary candy store to practice their money skills. To prepare this center, make several copies of the jar math mat (page 38) and a large supply of the candy and coin counters (page 39). Color the counters and math mats as desired; then cut apart the counters. Use some of the candy counters to create a price chart similar to the one shown. Glue combinations of the rest of the candy counters onto the jar mats. Then laminate the mats and the coin counters. To use this center, a student lays out all the candy jars. He checks the price list, then counts out the coins needed to buy each jar of candy. (You might have younger children use only pennies, whereas older students can use nickels and dimes, too.)

SMALL-GROUP ACTIVITY

Penny Candy Game

Here's another chance for children to use their purchasing power! Give each child a jar math mat and 15 penny counters. Drop a supply of candy counters in a real jar. Then display the price list created for "The Candy Store" (above). To play, each child, in turn, takes one candy from the jar. He consults the price list, then counts pennies from his jar to buy it. (If a child pulls out a candy he cannot afford, he puts it back in the jar and waits for his next turn.) Continue in this manner until each child has spent all of his money.

I can afford this!

MATH STORY PROBLEMS

Count on these ideas for filling your small-group math time!

- "Put five pennies in your jar. Find one coin that equals that amount." (counting, money skills)
- "Put six candies in your jar. Put in five more. How many do you have all together?" (counting, addition)
- "Put 12 candies in your jar. Pretend to eat four. How many are left?" (counting, subtraction)
- "How many candies will fit in your jar? Guess. Now fill your jar with candies. How many fit?" (estimation, counting)
- "Let's pretend that you have seven cents. Place coins that equal that amount in your jar." (counting, money skills)

ADD TO YOUR JAR

An empty jar is full of possibilities! Keep seasons and holidays in mind when you think of counters to use with your jar math mats. How about some of these?

- candy conversation hearts
- jelly beans
- candy corn
- peppermint discs
- buttons, real coins
- Cookie-Crisp® cereal

Jar Math Mat

Use with the activities on page 37.

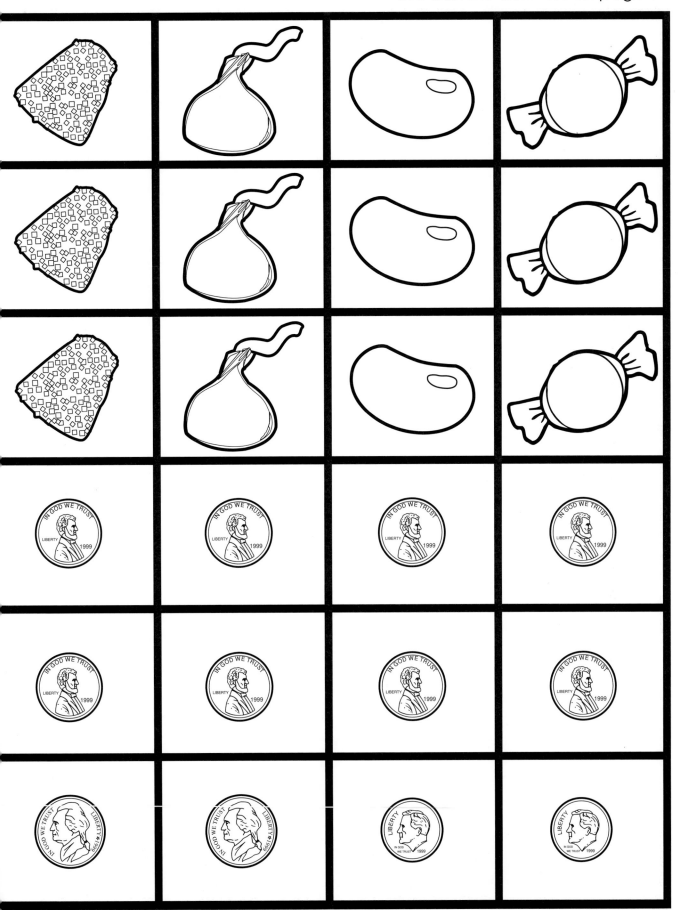

39

PIZZA'S HERE!

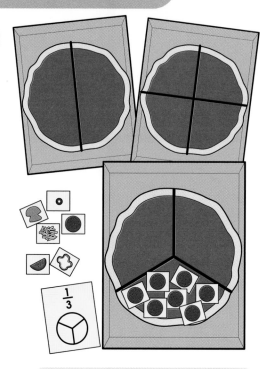

CENTER

Toppings to Go

This center is sliced just right to reinforce simple fractions. To prepare, make copies of the pizza math mat on page 41. Divide one of the pizzas into halves, one into thirds, and one into quarters. Next, make a large supply of the topping counters (page 42). Color and laminate the mats and counters; then cut apart the counters. Finally, make nine fraction cards: two showing $1/2$, three showing $1/3$, and four showing $1/4$. Add an illustration to each one for clarity.

To use this center, a child lays out the three mats and stacks the fraction cards facedown. Then she turns over one card, identifies the fraction, and finds the matching pizza. She adds the toppings of her choice to one slice of that particular pizza. Then she continues to turn over fraction cards until all the pizzas are fully topped.

SMALL-GROUP ACTIVITY

Let's Order Pizza!

Youngsters will keep these classroom customers satisfied by listening and counting very carefully. Provide each child in a small group with a pizza math mat and a supply of topping counters. Teach them the call-and-response chant below, giving each child a turn to do the ordering. Once an order is placed, have everyone in the group create a pizza to match the order.

Group: Hello. Hello.
What do you say?
What would you like on your pizza today?

Child: I'd like [seven mushrooms], please.

Group: Ready in a jiffy—guaranteed!

I'd like four olives, please!

MATH STORY PROBLEMS

Top off your small-group math times with these story problems.

- "Put four mushrooms on your pizza. Add three pepperoni slices. Add three green pepper slices. How many toppings do you have all together?" (counting, addition)
- "Put three slices of pepperoni on one half of your pizza. Make the other half match." (counting, fractions, matching sets)
- "Put ten slices of pepperoni on your pizza. Pretend to eat two of them. How many are left?" (counting, subtraction)

EXTRA TOPPINGS

What do you like on *your* pizza math mats? Try some of these ideas for alternative counters.

- red bingo chips for pepperoni
- small brown pom-poms for sausage
- small black beads for olives
- yellow yarn for cheese

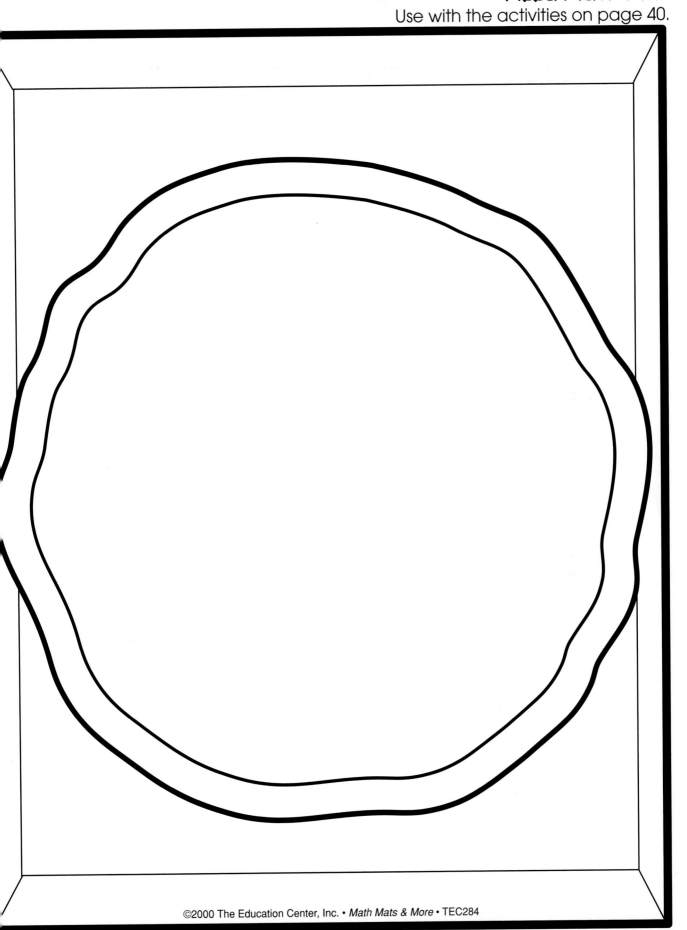

Pizza Topping Counters
Use with the activities on page 40.

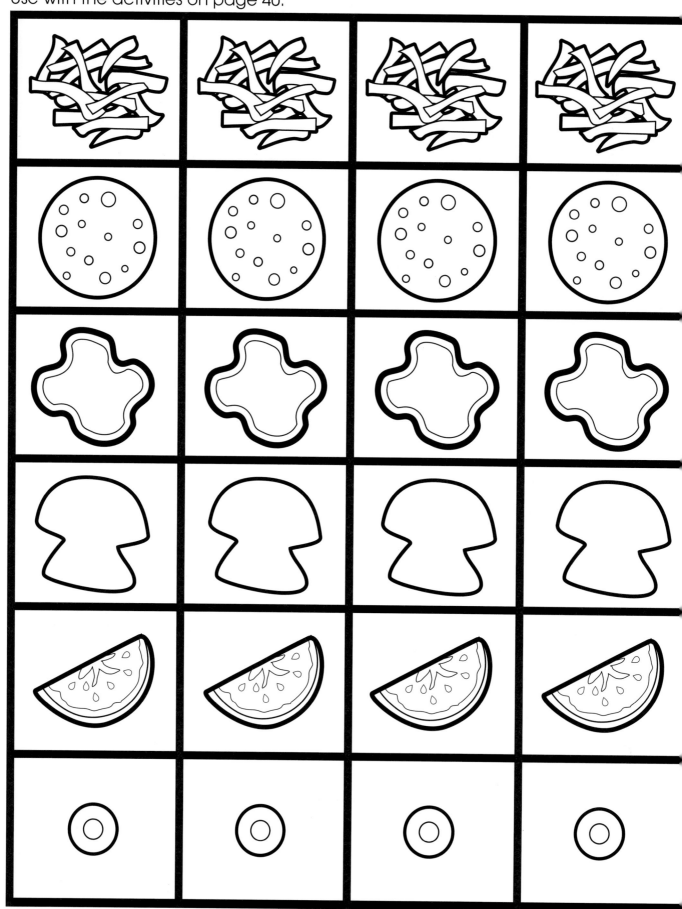

WHAT A TREASURE!

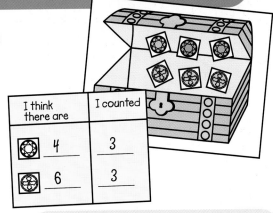

CENTER

Coins and Jewels Galore

Little treasure seekers can practice a bounty of math skills at this center! To prepare, decorate a small lidded box to resemble a treasure chest. Make a few treasure chest math mats (page 44) and a supply of the coin and jewel counters (page 45) as described on page 3. Put the counters in the treasure chest. Then, use a copy of a jewel and coin counter to make a supply of recording sheets similar to the one shown.

At this center, a child opens the treasure chest and takes a handful of treasure for his treasure chest mat. He estimates how many jewels and how many coins he has and writes the numbers on a recording sheet. Then he sorts the two types of treasure, counts each type, and records the actual number of each.

SMALL-GROUP ACTIVITY

Sunken Treasure

Teach a small group to play Sunken Treasure. They'll have a great time and get in some counting practice, too! To prepare, create a few diver cards, sized to match the jewel and coin counters on page 45. Mix the diver cards in with a large supply of the counters, and stack all the cards (counters) facedown. Give each child in a small group a treasure chest mat.

To play, each child, in turn, draws a card from the stack. If the card shows a coin or jewel, she places it in her treasure chest. If a player draws a diver card, she may take two additional cards from the pile. Play continues until all the treasure has been recovered. Then the players count their treasure to see who has the most!

MATH STORY PROBLEMS

What do teachers treasure? These great ideas for small-group math time, of course!

- "Put six coins and five jewels in your treasure chest. Do you have more coins or jewels? How many more?" (counting, comparing sets)

- "Put three coins in your treasure chest. Now trade each coin for two jewels. How many jewels do you have?" (skip counting, reasoning)

- "Put ten coins in your treasure chest. Pretend that three fall out. How many are left?" (counting, subtraction)

- "Put four jewels in your treasure chest. How many more do you think will fit? Guess. Then fill your chest and count." (estimation, counting)

A RICH BOUNTY

For more valuable learning, try some of these optional counters with your treasure chest math mats.

- wrapped chocolate coins
- plastic jewels
- toy jewelry
- small toys
- pennies, nickels, and dimes

Treasure Chest Math Mat

Use with the activities on page 43.

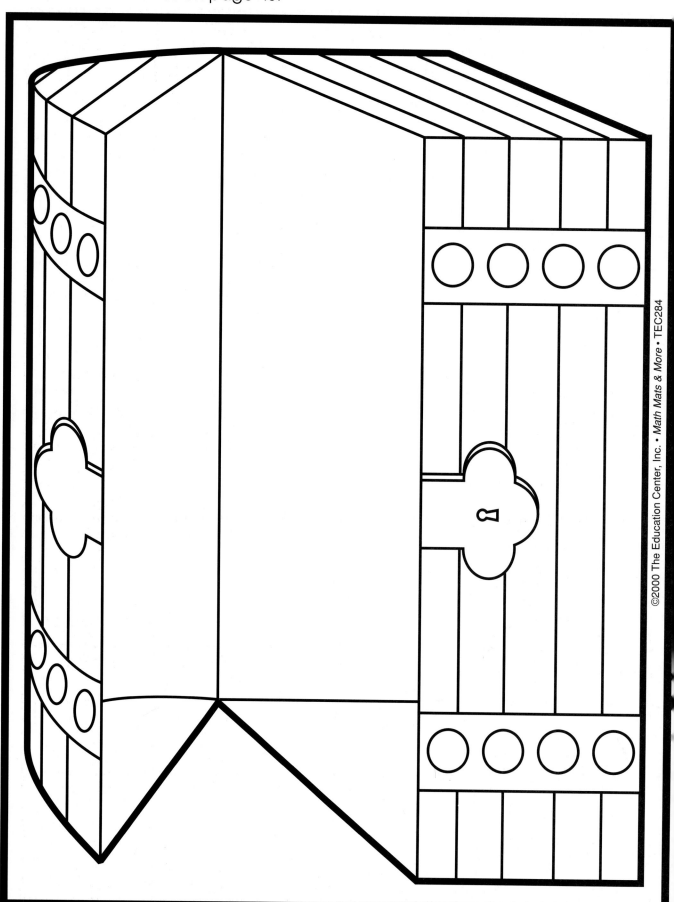

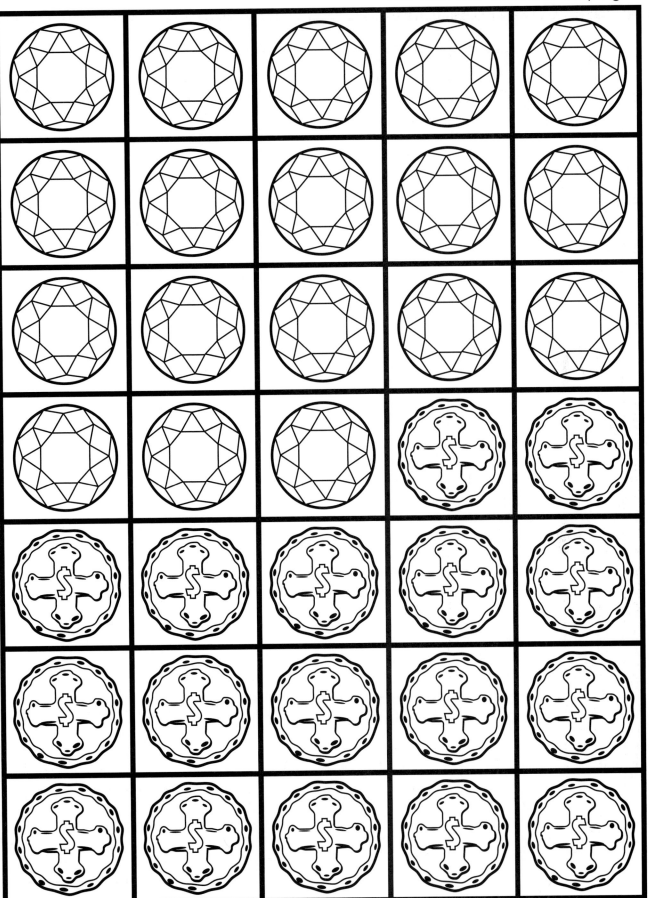

CRACKER CRAZY

CENTER

Cracker Sorting

Shape skills liven up with this cracker sorting center. To prepare, make four copies of the box math mat (on page 47) and a large supply of the cracker counters (on page 48) as described on page 3. Store the cracker counters in a real cracker box.

At this center, a child removes the cracker counters from the box, then sorts them by shape onto the four math mats. As a reward for a job well done, invite each child who completes this center to enjoy a treat of your class's favorite cracker snack mix.

SMALL-GROUP ACTIVITY

Spin a Cracker

This small-group game will have students spinning their way through shape recognition and matching skills! To prepare, make a simple seven-inch spinner including one copy of each of the cracker counters on page 48. Give each player a box math mat and ten randomly selected cracker counters to arrange on his mat.

To play, one child spins the spinner and finds the shape (from his mat) on which the spinner lands. He then removes one cracker of that shape from his box. The next child spins and repeats the process. Play continues until one child has emptied his box of crackers. When the game's over, it's time for a snack—crackers, of course!

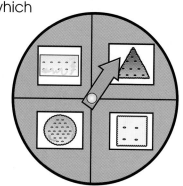

MATH STORY PROBLEMS

Mmm...how about these crunchy-munchy math story problems?

- "Put three triangle crackers in your box. Add two round crackers. How many crackers are in your box?" (counting, shapes, addition)

- "Put seven crackers in your box. Pretend to eat three. How many are left?" (counting, subtraction)

- "How many crackers will fit in your box? Guess. Now cover your box with crackers. How many fit?" (estimation, counting)

- "Use the crackers to make a pattern on your mat." (shapes, patterning)

A BOX FULL OF POSSIBILITIES

Of course, a box can hold many things besides crackers. Here are some ideas for alternative counters to use with your box math mats.

- dried pasta
- easy-to-handle cereal pieces (such as Cheerios® or Cookie-Crisp® cereal)
- jigsaw puzzle pieces
- animal crackers

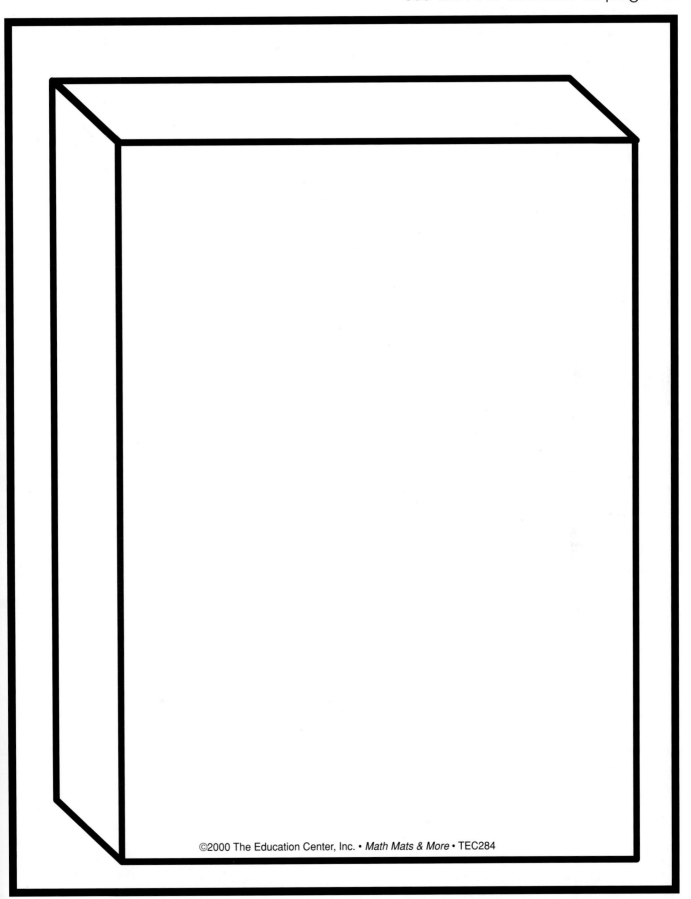

Cracker Counters

Use with the activities on page 46.

SOUP'S ON!

CENTER

What's Cooking?

Students will have a delicious time stirring up math skills in this simmering center! In advance, make a few soup pot math mats (page 50) and a large supply of counters (page 51) as described on page 3. Also prepare a supply of counters without laminating them. Use the unlaminated counters to make a set of recipe cards. For each card, glue a different combination of counters on an index card. Label the cards as shown; then store them in a recipe box. Put the recipe box and a bowl full of counters in a center along with the soup pot mats. To use this center, a child selects a recipe card, then follows the recipe by placing the exact ingredients (counters) in his own soup pot. Soup's on!

2 bow-tie noodles
1 tomato
1 bean

SMALL-GROUP ACTIVITY

"Souper" Chant

Heat up counting skills with this math activity. Begin by giving each child in the small group a math mat and a set of counters. Recite the chant below, inserting a different child's name in the last line each time. Ask that child to say what he would like to put in his soup, and have him put the appropriate counters in his pot. Then direct the rest of the children to put the same ingredients in their pots.

Stir it up,
Heat it up,
Eat it every day.
Here's how to make soup
   [Seth]'s way!

My soup has two tomatoes and one bean. Mmmm, good!

MATH STORY PROBLEMS

Make your small-group math times even more appetizing with these math story problems!

- "Put one tomato and one mushroom in your soup pot. How many ingredients do you have all together?" (counting, addition)

- "Put five noodles in your soup. Pretend to eat three. How many noodles are left?" (counting, subtraction)

- "Put two noodles in your pot. Add five beans. Which has more? How many more?" (counting, comparing sets)

MORE, PLEASE

Keep your soup pot math mats bubbling with these alternative counters.

- dry pasta
- dry alphabet pasta
- small soup crackers
- dried beans
- small toy vegetables (available at craft stores)

Soup Pot Math Mat

Use with the activities on page 49.

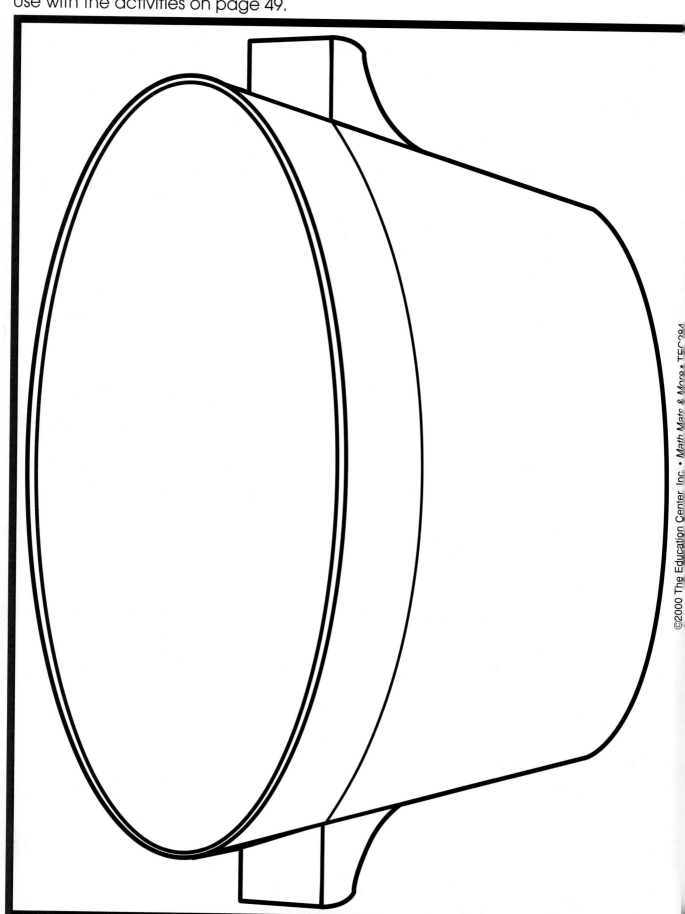

YUM! GUM!

CENTER

Pennies or Gumballs

No child can resist the sweet and colorful draw of a gumball machine! To prepare this gumball-buying center, make a gumball machine math mat (page 53) and a supply of the gumball and coin counters (page 54) as described on page 3. Glue varying numbers of the penny counters to index cards. (For older students, use the nickel counters as well.) Then laminate the cards before placing them in a wallet. To use this center, a child lays the gumball machine math mat on the table and "fills" it with a supply of gumballs. She then opens the wallet and takes out a card. She "buys" the number of gumballs to match the amount of money shown on the card. She continues until her pennies or the gumballs are gone. Which will it be?

SMALL-GROUP ACTIVITY

Fill 'er Up

Counting skills will be on a roll with this game of chance. Give each child in a small group a gumball machine math mat and ten gumball counters, placed facedown in his machine. To play, each child, in turn, rolls a die and then turns over the corresponding number of gumballs. Play continues until one child has turned over all his gumballs and "filled" his machine. The winner gets the honor of passing out a gumball (or other age-appropriate treat) to each of his fellow players before taking one for himself. Your students will want to play this game again and again—guaranteed!

MATH STORY PROBLEMS

Use these story problems to get your small-group math times going!

- "Put three red gumballs in your machine. Add two blue gumballs. Add five yellow gumballs. Which color has the most? The fewest?" (counting, comparing sets)

- "Put nine gumballs in your machine. Buy three gumballs (take them out). How many are left?" (counting, subtraction)

- "Put five-cent gumballs in your machine. You have two nickels. How many gumballs can you buy?" (counting, money skills)

- "Put eight one-cent gumballs in your machine. Find coins to equal the amount you need to buy all of them." (money skills)

FURTHER FUN FILLERS

Pop these counters into your gumball machine math mats for a change of pace.

- pom-pom gumballs
- individually wrapped pieces of bubble gum
- Runts® candies
- Chiclets® gum
- tiny toys
- candy mini stickers on pennies

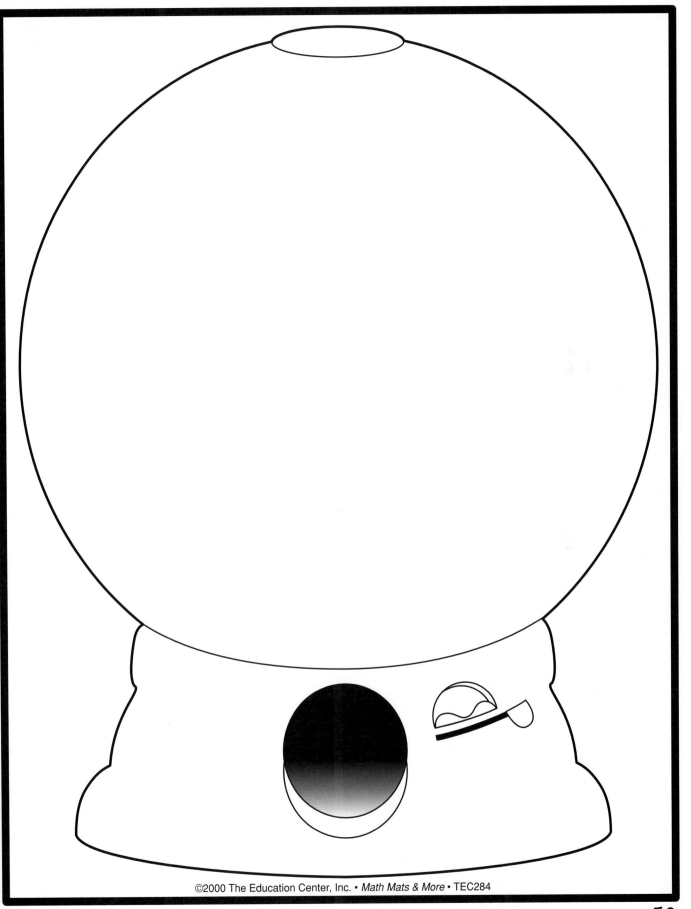

Gumball and Coin Counters
Use with the activities on page 52.

TOOL TIME!

CENTER

Measuring Up

Help little ones nail down measurement skills with this sorting center. To prepare, make a toolbox math mat (page 56) and a large supply of nail counters (page 57) as described on page 3. In a center, set up three small baskets, labeled as shown. Store the counters in a toy toolbox if available.

To use this center, a child measures each nail using the ruler provided on the toolbox math mat. She then sorts the nails into the three baskets.

SMALL-GROUP ACTIVITY

Time for Tools!

Build students' measurement and addition skills with this small-group game. To prepare, place a large supply of nail counters in a basket. Then make a set of cards, each showing the numeral 1, 2, or 3. Stack the cards facedown in the center of the table. Then give each child a toolbox math mat and four different tool counters from page 57. Have each player turn her tool counters facedown on her mat.

To play, a child draws a card and reads the numeral. She takes a corresponding number of nails from the basket and measures them to find the total length of all the nails. Once she has discovered the total, she turns over one of her tools. When a player has all four of her tools faceup, she calls out "Tool time!"

Tool time!

MATH STORY PROBLEMS

These story problems really measure up when it comes to making the most of your small-group math time!

- "In your toolbox, put one hammer, one wrench, and two screwdrivers. How many tools do you have all together?" (counting, addition)

- "You have a two-inch nail. You need a nail that is two inches longer. Measure and find the nail you need." (measurement skills, addition)

- "Measure your hammer and your pliers. Which is longer?" (measurement skills)

- "Put 12 nails in your toolbox. Take out 6 to fix something. How many are left?" (counting, subtraction)

OTHER HANDY COUNTERS

Try using some of these alternative counters with your toolbox math mats.

- plastic pegs
- metal washers
- nuts and bolts
- craft sticks cut to different lengths (lumber)

Toolbox Math Mat

Use with the activities on page 55.

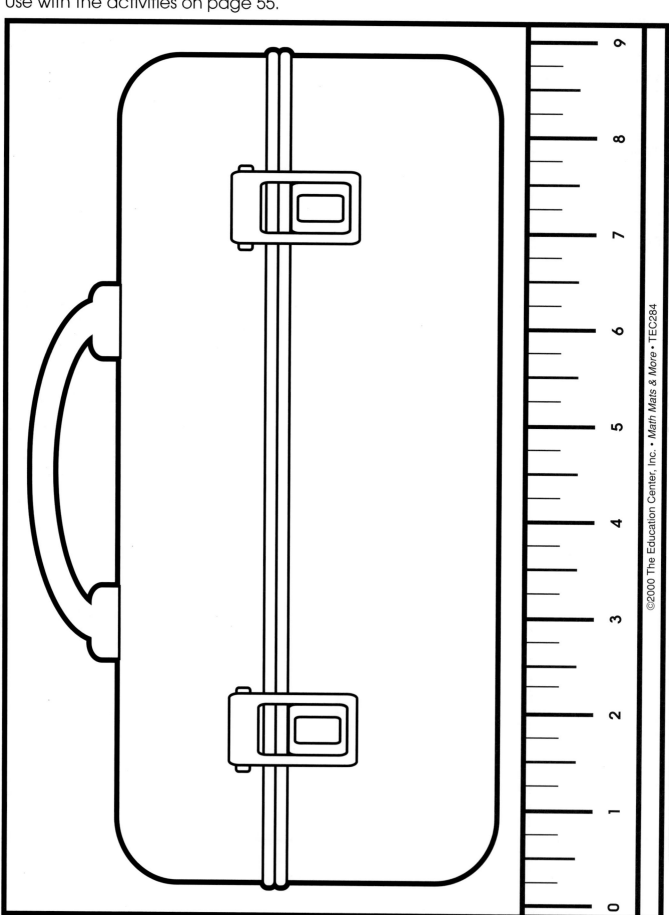

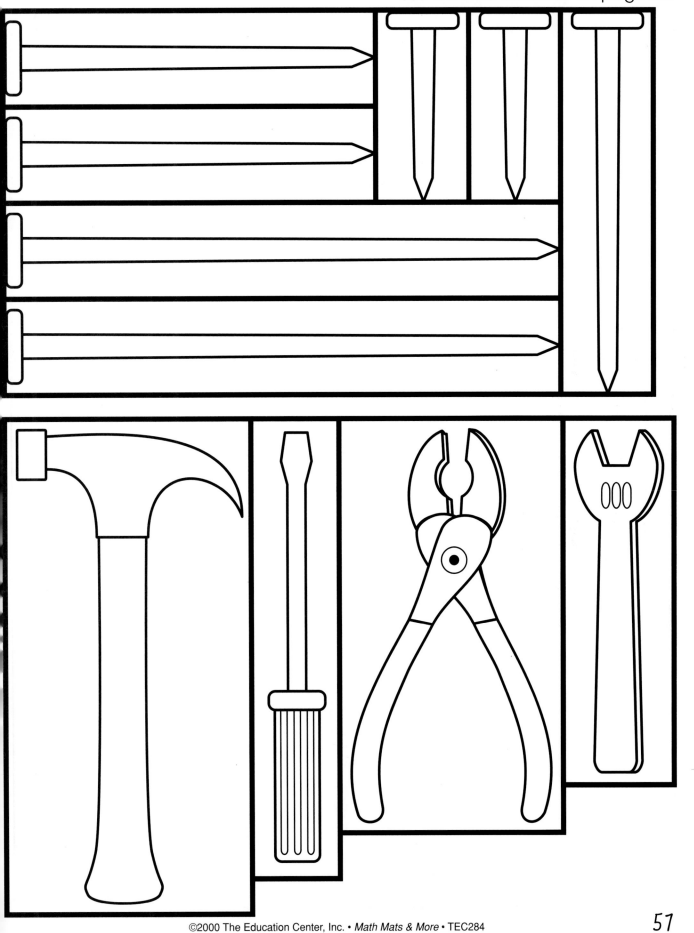

DOWN ON THE FARM!

CENTER

Order in the Farmyard

Set up this center to assess your students' grasp of ordinal numbers. To prepare, seal a small box with tape; then glue a copy of each animal counter on page 60 onto a different side of the cube. Also make a farm math mat (on page 59) and a supply of the farm animal counters (on page 60) as described on page 3. At this center, a child rolls the animal die. She places a corresponding animal counter next to the barn door. Then she rolls again, placing the next animal rolled in line next to the first one. When she has five animals in line by the barn door, ask her to identify which animal is second, fourth, first, etc.

SMALL-GROUP ACTIVITY

Where, Oh, Where Do the Animals Go?

Focus on positional words with this musical small-group activity. To begin, make a supply of cards with positional phrases written on them. Stack the phrase cards facedown. Then give each child a farm math mat and a supply of farm animal counters. Have each child hold up an animal counter and sing the song below. Then ask one child to draw a phrase card. Read the card aloud; then encourage each child to place his animal counter in the corresponding position on his mat. Keep going until every child has had a turn or two to pick a phrase card.

(sung to the tune of "Where, Oh, Where Has My Little Dog Gone?")

above the
flowers

between the
barn and the
fence

Where, oh, where does this animal go?
Where, oh, where should it be?
On or under or in between?
Let's read a card, and we'll see!

in front of
the barn

under the
cloud

next to
the fence

on the silo

MATH STORY PROBLEMS

Keep your small-group math time "moo-ving" right along with these farm story problems!

- "Put one cow on your mat. Add two ducks and three chickens. How many animals are in the barnyard?" (counting, addition)

- "Five chickens were in the barnyard. Two walked away. How many were left?" (counting, subtraction)

ADDITIONAL ANIMAL COUNTERS
Keep little ones quacking about your farm math mats by using some of these alternative counters.

- small toy farm animals
- farm animal mini erasers
- farm animal mini stickers on pennies
- colored pom-poms or chips to represent animals (pink pigs, yellow chicks, etc.)

Farm Animal Counters
Use with the activities on page 58.